OSV Kids Stations of the Cross

Stations
of the **Cross**

Written by Colleen Pressprich • Illustrated by Adalee Hude

Huntington, Indiana

Nihil Obstat
Msgr. Michael Heintz, Ph.D.
Censor Librorum

Imprimatur
✠ Kevin C. Rhoades
Bishop of Fort Wayne-South Bend
October 12, 2021

The *Nihil Obstat* and *Imprimatur* are official declarations that a book is free from doctrinal or moral error. It is not implied that those who have granted the *Nihil Obstat* and *Imprimatur* agree with the contents, opinions, or statements expressed.

Our Sunday Visitor Publishing Division

Our Sunday Visitor, Inc.
200 Noll Plaza
Huntington, IN 46750
1-800-348-2440

ISBN: 978-1-68192-987-3 (Inventory No. T2722)
JUVENILE NONFICTION—Religious—Christian—Devotional & Prayer.
JUVENILE NONFICTION—Holidays & Celebrations—Easter & Lent.
RELIGION—Christianity—Catholic.

LCCN: 2021947969

Cover and interior design: Lindsey Riesen
Cover and interior art: Adalee Hude

PRINTED IN THE UNITED STATES OF AMERICA

Dear Parents, Teachers, and Priests,

The Stations of the Cross can feel like a difficult topic to approach with children. I've written these stations in language that children will understand and connect with to help make it easier to teach them about the passion of Christ. I have found in my work with children that they are naturally drawn to the suffering Christ. They have an innate capacity to empathize, and a natural ability to internalize faith even at a very young age.

At the end of each meditation in this booklet, I have included a few questions, which are meant to be a jumping-off point for you to discuss that station with children. Sometimes children are unable or unwilling to discuss their thoughts, and they will not offer any response to a question. Rather than quickly moving past it, this can be a wonderful opportunity for you to model sharing faith by talking about your own experiences. Do not be surprised if the child loops back to the topic later on in the day.

With Prayers,

Colleen Pressprich

Introduction for Children

When we pray the Stations of the Cross, we remember each step along Jesus' journey to save us. We spend time thinking about how he felt as he carried his cross, and as he died for each of us. This helps us love him better, and learn from his example. Most importantly, it shows us just how much love he has for us.

The Stations

†

First Station: Jesus Is Condemned to Death

Second Station: Jesus Takes Up His Cross

Third Station: Jesus Falls the First Time

Fourth Station: Jesus Meets His Mother

Fifth Station: Simon Helps Jesus Carry the Cross

Sixth Station: Veronica Wipes the Face of Jesus

Seventh Station: Jesus Falls the Second Time

Eighth Station: Jesus Meets the Women of Jerusalem

Ninth Station: Jesus Falls the Third Time

Tenth Station: Jesus Is Stripped of His Clothes

Eleventh Station: Jesus Is Nailed to the Cross

Twelfth Station: Jesus Dies on the Cross

Thirteenth Station: Jesus Is Taken Down from the Cross

Fourteenth Station: Jesus Is Laid in the Tomb

Jesus Is Condemned to Death

Leader: We adore you, O Christ, and we praise you.

Child: Because, by your holy cross, you have redeemed the world.

Jesus is alone before Pontius Pilate. All his disciples have left him. No one is there to stand up for him. He doesn't shout or argue when he is condemned to death, even though he is innocent. Instead, he accepts the decision of Pilate without complaint. He is quiet and calm.

Have you ever felt alone? Were you scared?
What do you think made Jesus able to remain peaceful in front of Pilate? Why do you think that he didn't argue?

Pray
Dear Jesus, help us to remember that no matter where we are, we are never alone. You are always with us. Amen.

Jesus Takes Up His Cross

Leader: We adore you, O Christ, and we praise you.

Child: Because, by your holy cross, you have redeemed the world.

The soldiers make Jesus carry his own cross to the hill where he will die. The cross is very heavy. Jesus was in prison all night, and he hasn't eaten any food since the Last Supper the night before. He has also been beaten. He is tired and weak, yet he still chooses to take up his own cross and walk toward his death because he loves us.

Have you ever had to do something very hard even though you were tired? How did it feel? What helped you keep going? What do you think Jesus was thinking when he lifted the heavy cross onto his back?

Pray

Dear Jesus, please remind us that you are with us when we are tired and don't want to do what is asked of us. Please help us to remember that we can offer up what we don't like as a prayer. Amen.

Jesus Falls the First Time

Leader: We adore you, O Christ, and we praise you.

Child: Because, by your holy cross, you have redeemed the world.

The cross is so heavy. Jesus is weak with hunger. He is exhausted, sweaty, and dirty. He falls down on the rough street, in front of all the watching crowds. But what happens next is what we should pay attention to: Jesus gets back up! He chooses to keep going. Even though he is so tired and hurt, he lifts the cross onto his back and starts again.

Have you ever fallen or made a mistake in front of other people? How did you feel?
What do you think Jesus felt when he fell in front of the crowds? Why do you think he got back up?

Pray
Dear Jesus, you could have chosen to save yourself. But instead you allowed yourself to fall under the weight of your cross. Thank you for showing us that you know how we feel when we fall or find something difficult. Thank you for showing us how to get back up. Amen.

Jesus Meets His Mother

Leader: We adore you, O Christ, and we praise you.

Child: Because, by your holy cross, you have redeemed the world.

Mary is always there for Jesus. When his friends leave him alone, she stays close by. Even though it is heartbreaking for her to watch, she stays close by to encourage Jesus as he carries the cross. Mary makes sure that he can see her and feel her presence.

She does all this because he is her child, and she loves him. We are also Mary's children, which means that this Station also shows us how much Mary loves us. She will never leave us, either.

What do you think Jesus felt when he saw his mom?
What do you think Mary said to him when they met?
Do you ever talk to Mary?

Pray
Dear Jesus, thank you for giving us Mary as our mother, too. Help us to love her the way you do and to trust her when we are in trouble. Amen.

Simon Helps Jesus Carry the Cross

Leader: We adore you, O Christ, and we praise you.

Child: Because, by your holy cross, you have redeemed the world.

Helping a criminal carry his cross was not a part of Simon's plan for the day. But the soldiers guarding Jesus pull Simon from the crowd to do just that. At first he is angry, but then he looks at the bleeding man next to him. He sees the love and pain in Jesus' eyes. Then Simon shoulders the cross and is glad to be able to help Jesus.

Have you ever had the chance to help someone but didn't want to? How did you feel?
What do you think Simon thought when he was pulled from the crowd? How do you think he felt after he had helped Jesus?

Pray
Dear Jesus, please give us the grace to help other people, even when we don't want to. Help us to pay attention when our brothers, sisters, or friends need us. Help us to respond to them with love. Amen.

Veronica Wipes the Face of Jesus

Leader: We adore you, O Christ, and we praise you.

Child: Because, by your holy cross, you have redeemed the world.

Veronica pushes through the crowds until she is right at the front. She sees the soldiers and grows afraid, but then she sees Jesus. Her love for him drowns out all her fear. She runs up to him, ignoring everything and everyone else. She uses her veil to wipe the blood, sweat, and tears from Jesus' face. Her simple act of love makes it easier for him to keep going.

Are there people who show you love when you are hurt?
How does it make you feel?
Is there a person in your life who needs encouragement?
How can you show that person love?

Pray
Dear Jesus, thank you for the people who help and encourage us when we are doing something difficult. Help us to remember to be like them when we see family or friends who need someone to cheer them on. Amen.

Jesus Falls the Second Time

Leader: We adore you, O Christ, and we praise you.

Child: Because, by your holy cross, you have redeemed the world.

The weight of the cross is too much for Jesus. He falls down again. He is tired. His whole body aches. But he knows he must get up. Because of his love for you and me, he chooses to get up again. He chooses to keep going and to carry his cross.

Did you know what while Jesus carries his cross, he is thinking of all of the people he loves — including you? This love is what keeps him going, but he has to choose it. Sometimes we don't feel like loving. Sometimes we feel tired or cranky. But we can ask Jesus to help us choose to be kind, patient, and loving in those moments.

Can you think of a time when it was difficult for you to choose to love? What helped you then?

Pray
Dear Jesus, show us how to choose to love even when we don't feel like it. Help us to love like you. Amen.

Jesus Meets the Women of Jerusalem

Leader: We adore you, O Christ, and we praise you.

Child: Because, by your holy cross, you have redeemed the world.

Along the way of the cross, Jesus meets some of the women of the city. He has met many of these women before. They heard him preach and teach. Today they are crying at the sight of his pain. But Jesus isn't thinking of himself. He tells the women not to cry for him, because he is doing the will of his Father. Instead, he tells them to cry for people who are sinning. They are the people who really need help.

Are there any people in the world today who might need God's help? Who can you pray for today?

Pray

Dear Jesus, thank you for reminding us to pray for our world. Please be with those who continue to sin. Help them to repent and follow you. Amen.

Jesus Falls the Third Time

Leader: We adore you, O Christ, and we praise you.

Child: Because, by your holy cross, you have redeemed the world.

As he carries the cross, Jesus falls a third time. The soldiers yell at him, but no one comes to help him stand up and lift the heavy cross again. He doesn't complain or get angry. He forgives the soldiers, and he loves them anyway.

Have you ever had a hard time forgiving a sibling or friend who has hurt you?
Have you ever gotten angry when you didn't succeed at something right away and needed to keep trying?

Pray
Dear Jesus, please help us to forgive the people who hurt us. And please help us to remember to keep trying when we have a difficult job to do. Help us to work hard without complaining or whining. Amen.

TENTH STATION

Jesus Is Stripped of His Clothes

Leader: We adore you, O Christ, and we praise you.

Child: Because, by your holy cross, you have redeemed the world.

When Jesus finally arrives at the top of Calvary, the soldiers want to embarrass him and make him feel ashamed. So they take off his clothes.

Long ago, in the Garden of Eden, Adam and Eve felt ashamed because they realized they were naked after they sinned. They hid from God. But Jesus doesn't feel ashamed, and he doesn't hide. He knows that the Father loves him. He wants to show us that we don't have to feel ashamed in front of God.

Have you ever felt ashamed after doing something wrong? What did you do?

Pray

Dear Jesus, please help us to remember that we don't need to hide from you. Remind us to run to you when we need help, even if we feel embarrassed or ashamed. Amen.

Jesus Is Nailed to the Cross

Leader: We adore you, O Christ, and we praise you.

Child: Because, by your holy cross, you have redeemed the world.

The soldiers hammer nails into Jesus' hands and feet. He is in more pain than ever. But he still doesn't yell or get angry. Instead, he prays out loud, asking his Father to forgive the soldiers and the people who want to kill him. He loves even though he is hurting.

It can be hard to love when you're in pain. Have you ever gotten so hurt that it made you grumpy? What did you do? How can you love like Jesus even when you're hurting?

Pray

Dear Jesus, help me to love others even when I am in pain. Be there to comfort all those who are sick and in pain today. Amen.

Jesus Dies on the Cross

Leader: We adore you, O Christ, and we praise you.

Child: Because, by your holy cross, you have redeemed the world.

When Jesus dies on the cross, the ground starts to shake. The sky becomes dark, even though it is still daytime. The people who had wanted Jesus to die become very, very scared. Some of them realize that they made a mistake. Jesus was innocent! They now believe that he is the Son of God and are sorry for what they have done. And God forgives them.

Is it hard for you to admit when you make mistakes? What can you do if you make a mistake?

Pray

Dear Jesus, please help me when I make mistakes. Help me to apologize and to try to fix it. Amen.

Jesus Is Taken Down from the Cross

Leader: We adore you, O Christ, and we praise you.

Child: Because, by your holy cross, you have redeemed the world.

Jesus has died. His body is taken down from the cross. Mary cradles him in her arms. John and Mary Magdalene, his good friends, sob because Jesus is dead. They feel as if their whole world has ended. They don't know what is going to happen next. Sometimes it can feel like everything in our world is wrong. We don't always understand what God is doing. Those are the times when we need to remember to have faith. God loves us. He is with us.

Have you ever had a time when you felt like everything was wrong? What did you do then?

Pray

Dear Jesus, help us to remember that you are with us even when it feels like everything is going wrong. Keep us strong in faith like Mary your mother. Amen.

Jesus Is Laid in the Tomb

Leader: We adore you, O Christ, and we praise you.

Child: Because, by your holy cross, you have redeemed the world.

A rich man named Joseph of Arimathea gives Jesus his own tomb, and the disciples lay him in it. Then they roll a big rock over the entrance to seal the tomb shut. To them, this seems like the end of the story.

But we know what happens next. Jesus will rise from the dead on Easter Sunday!

Why do you think Joseph of Arimathea offered his tomb for Jesus? How do you think the disciples felt when they saw the rock rolled over the tomb's entrance?
How do you think Mary felt?

Pray
Thank you, Jesus, for dying on the cross so that we could join you in heaven. Thank you for rising from the dead and bringing us new life. We love you. Amen.

About the Author

A former missionary and former Montessori teacher, Colleen seeks to use the lessons she learned in the mission field and the classroom to live her dream of homeschooling and building the domestic church. Colleen lives with her husband, children, and grandmother in Michigan, where they enjoy everything about spring, summer, and fall, and hate  the winters. She is the author of *Marian Consecration for Families with Young Children* (OSV, 2020), *Women Doctors of the Church* (OSV, 2022), and *The Jesse Tree for Families* (OSV, 2022).

About the Illustrator

Adalee Hude has been studying art all her life. She earned a BA in art from Cal State Long Beach. She was called from a career in secular art to focus on Catholic sacred art and writing. Her artistic repertoire includes painting, sculpture, illustration, design, and crafting. The Arts & Crafts movement,  medieval art, and God's beautiful world are particular influences on her work, as are the lives of the saints. Her work is available on her website, www.brightlyhude.com.